Hueber Lektüren

Englisch

The Little Roxy Cinema

LEKTÜRE MIT AUDIOS ONLINE

Denise Kirby
Illustrated by Szilvia Szakall

Hueber Verlag

This is the German version of **The Little Roxy Cinema**

The Little Roxy Cinema

ILTS Created and developed by
International Language Teaching Services Ltd
First floor, 1 Market Street
Saffron Walden, Essex CB10 1JB, UK

help@ilts.info
www.ilts.info

Author: Denise Kirby
Series editor: James Bean
Illustrations: Szilvia Szakall
Text design: ILTS Ltd
Origination: e-BookServices.com
Audio production: Mike Raggett, Verbalists; Mark Smith, Tally Ho Studio
Voice actor: Mandy Weston

Der Verlag weist ausdrücklich darauf hin, dass im Text enthaltene externe Links vom Verlag nur bis zum Zeitpunkt der Buchveröffentlichung eingesehen werden konnten. Auf spätere Veränderungen hat der Verlag keinerlei Einfluss. Eine Haftung des Verlags ist daher ausgeschlossen.

Das Werk und seine Teile sind urheberrechtlich geschützt. Jede Verwertung in anderen als den gesetzlich zugelassenen Fällen bedarf deshalb der vorherigen schriftlichen Einwilligung des Verlags.

Eingetragene Warenzeichen oder Marken sind Eigentum des jeweiligen Zeichen- bzw. Markeninhabers, auch dann, wenn diese nicht gekennzeichnet sind. Es ist jedoch zu beachten, dass weder das Vorhandensein noch das Fehlen derartiger Kennzeichnungen die Rechtslage hinsichtlich dieser gewerblichen Schutzrechte berührt.

3.	2.	1.		Die letzten Ziffern
2024	23	22	21 20	bezeichnen Zahl und Jahr des Druckes.

Alle Drucke dieser Auflage können, da unverändert,
nebeneinander benutzt werden.
1. Auflage
Copyright © 2020 International Language Teaching Services Ltd
© 2020 Hueber Verlag GmbH & Co. KG, München, Deutschland
Umschlaggestaltung: Sieveking · Agentur für Kommunikation, München
Umschlagfoto: © Getty Images/iStock/zsv3207
Verlagsredaktion: Heike Birner, Hueber Verlag, München
Druck und Bindung: Passavia Druckservice GmbH & Co. KG, Passau
Printed in Germany
ISBN 978–3–19–202997–4

Contents

Chapter 1	Film club	▶ 7	4
Chapter 2	The old shop	▶ 8	8
Chapter 3	Is it a ghost?	▶ 9	12
Chapter 4	Nice and quiet	▶ 10	16
Chapter 5	Let's get out of here!	▶ 11	20
Activities		▶ 3-6	24
Glossary			32
Key			35

▶ Das Hörbuch zur Lektüre und die Tracks zu den Übungen stehen als kostenloser MP3-Download bereit unter:
www.hueber.de/audioservice
Zugangscode: ea980ba0ez

Chapter 1
Film club

'I can't see the picture,' says Angus. 'I can only see the back of your head, Marnie. Move.'

I move over, near Ava.

'Now *I* can't see,' says Lily. 'Marnie, your head is too big.'

We are watching a film. There's me, Lily, Ava, Angus, Ray and Joel. And my dad.

On Friday nights, we have a film club. Tonight we're watching a film from the 1950s, *The 5000 Fingers of Dr T*.

We like old films. Sometimes we laugh at them. Sometimes they're very good.

My dad has hundreds of old films. He collects them. He collects old film projectors too. But my mum doesn't like them. 'I don't want those dusty things in my house,' she says. Dad keeps them in the garden shed – with the garden tools, flower pots, old shoes, bicycles … We have to watch the films in the shed too. That's okay for Dad and me. But now my friends come to the Film Club, and the shed is too small.

'Your head is too big, Marnie,' Lily says to me again.

'No, it's not,' I say. 'This shed is too small.'

'Yeah,' says Angus. 'We need a bigger shed. With nice chairs. And carpet on the floor. And popcorn to eat and –'

'Isn't that a cinema?' asks Dad.

'Oh, yeah,' says Angus and everyone laughs.

'We need a proper little cinema,' says Ava. 'Nice and clean. With no flower pots or old shoes in it.'

'Maybe it's not a bad idea,' says Dad.

I look at Ava and she looks at me.

'Yeah,' says Ava. 'Maybe it's a *good* idea.'

'Huh?' says Angus.

Everyone stops watching the film.

'Maybe it's a *great* idea,' I say. 'We can put nice chairs in it and give it a name and –'

'We can watch your films there too,' says Ava.

I like making short films. Ava always wants to be in them. She does karate and wants to be an action star.

'Yeah, let's do it,' says Lily. 'Let's make a proper cinema.'

'Yeah,' I say. I love the idea.

'But where?' asks Joel. 'We don't have a place.'

'Maybe you can ask Mr Sims,' says Dad. 'Maybe he has an empty building.'

Old Mr Sims lives down the road from us. He has a lot of old houses and shops in our town. But he's not very nice.

'I'm not going to see Mr Sims,' says Lily. 'I don't like his house – it's creepy.'

'Yeah,' says Ray. 'I'm not going. He always shouts at me.'

'I'll go,' I say.

'And I'll go,' says Angus. He jumps up. 'A proper cinema. What a great idea! *My* great idea! Yeah – "The Angus McTavish Cinema".'

Joel throws an old shoe at him and everyone laughs.

On Saturday morning, Angus and I go to see Mr Sims. He doesn't want to talk to us.

He throws open a window and shouts at us. 'What do you want?'

'Er ... hello, Mr Sims,' I say. 'Um ... I'm Marnie ... from down the road.'

'Yes, yes, yes. What do you want?'

'We have a film club and ... um ... we want to ask you ... um –'

'You have ten seconds,' says Mr Sims.

'Talk quickly!' Angus says to me.

'Can you help us? We have a film club and we have to watch the films in my garden shed, and it's very small, and we want a cinema, and –'

'I don't have a cinema,' says Mr Sims.

'No,' I say. 'We want to *make* a cinema. Do you have an empty building?'

'You want one of my buildings?'

'Only a small one,' says Angus.

'To watch films?'

'Yes!' says Angus.

Mr Sims shuts the window – BANG!

'The films are very good,' Angus shouts at the window. '*Animal Farm,* um ... *Superman and the Mole Men, The 5000 Fingers of Dr T* –'

The window opens again and Mr Sims puts his head out.

'*The 5000 Fingers of Dr T?*' he says. 'I remember that film. I remember the cinema on Saturday mornings ... with my brother ... I remember seeing that film. It's old.'

'We like old films,' I say.

'Humph ...' Mr Sims looks at us. 'There is an empty shop, down on Moorbrook Street.' He puts his hands up to close the window. 'Stay there, I have to look for the key.'

Chapter 2
The old shop

'Thirty-four Moorbrook Street,' says Angus. 'There it is.'

We go across the street and I put the key in the door. But it doesn't open. 'The key won't turn.'

'Here,' says Angus. 'I can do it.' He takes the key out and puts it in again. The key turns. He opens the door and we go in.

The place is very dirty. There's a dusty counter with shelves behind it. There are shelves along the walls too. The windows are black and there's rubbish on the floor – letters and newspapers and plastic bags. I can see two old cups and a dirty sock.

'What a mess!' says Angus. 'Look at this rubbish.' With two fingers, he takes a black thing off the counter. 'What's this?'

'Maybe an apple?' I say.

'Yuk.' Angus puts it down again.

I see the front page of a newspaper on the floor. It's old and yellow.

'Look at this paper,' I say. 'It's from Thursday, November the fifth, 1987.'

Angus opens a door at the back. 'There's a bathroom here,' he shouts. 'It's a mess.'

'Yeah, but this place is good. And we can clean it,' I shout. 'We can start this afternoon.' I take out my phone. 'Let's call everyone.'

Angus comes in.

'Hey,' I say. 'I've got a great idea. Let's have a sleepover.'

At two o'clock that afternoon, Dad drives me to the shop. I have my sleeping bag, a bag of food, a mop, a bucket and cleaning things.

I open the door and go in.

'Marnie!'

I hear a shout and Ava runs in. She has a rucksack on her back.

She looks at the room. 'Is this our little cinema?'

'It's a mess now,' I say. 'But we can make it nice.'

Ava puts down the rucksack, runs to me and gives me a hug. 'It's going to be cool! Where do we start?'

I get the bucket. 'Let's clean the windows.'

'Is everyone coming?'

'Not Ray and Lily. They're playing football. But Joel and Angus are coming.'

'Hey!' Joel is at the door but he's looking down the street. 'Marnie, Ava, come and look at this.'

Ava and I go to see. Angus is coming up the street. He has a mop and a broom, a sleeping bag, two plastic bags, a torch, a feather duster and a bucket on his head!

He holds the feather duster in the air. 'Where do we start?' he shouts.

We clean the windows and the shelves. We sweep up the rubbish and put it in bags. We wash the floor and clean the bathroom.

At six o'clock, Angus throws his sleeping bag onto the floor and sits on it. 'Can we stop now? I'm hungry.'

I put two big bags of rubbish near the door. 'Yeah, let's stop. I'm hungry too. And it's getting dark. I'm going to turn on the light.'

But the light doesn't turn on. I look up. There's no light bulb. 'Uh-oh, we don't have light.'

'It's okay,' says Angus. 'I have a torch.'

'And I have my phone,' says Joel.

'Yeah, me too,' I say.

We sit on our sleeping bags on the floor and everyone shares their food. Night comes and, in the torch light, we eat and laugh and talk ... and talk ... and talk.

I'm cold and I climb into my sleeping bag. I look at my phone. It's only nine o'clock but I'm tired.

Angus turns off the torch. The only light comes from a street lamp. The shop is dark and very quiet.

'Ooh, creepy,' he says. 'Woooooooo.'

'An-gus,' says Ava.

I shut my eyes. Ava and Joel are talking quietly.

'Hey, can you hear that?' says Angus.

'What?' asks Joel.

'That creepy sound. Listen.'

I laugh quietly.

'An-gus,' says Ava again. 'Stop it.'

'No,' says Angus. 'Listen.'

Everyone is quiet.

'Can you hear it?' he asks.

I sit up. 'Shh.'

And I hear the sound.

Chapter 3
Is it a ghost?

Something is scratching.

I grab my phone and turn on the light. 'What *is* that sound?'

'Is it a rat?' says Joel. 'Are there rats here? I don't like rats!'

'Shh,' says Angus.

We listen and hear the sound again. *Scrrr-atch*.

Angus turns on the torch. 'It's coming from behind the counter.' He gets up.

Joel grabs the torch. 'Yeah. But what is it?' He shines the light on the floor, at our sleeping bags, into my face.

'Joel!' I put a hand up to my eyes and climb out of my sleeping bag.

The light moves to the counter. 'Maybe it's a ghost,' says Joel.

Everyone is up now. 'Go and look,' says Ava.

'*You* go,' says Joel.

I shine my phone light at the floor and walk behind the counter. Everyone is quiet. We listen.

Scrrr-atch.

'The sound is coming from behind the shelves in the corner,' I say. 'Something's behind the shelves.'

'Can we move them?' asks Angus. Everyone comes over.

'Hey, I'm going to film this,' I say.

Joel shines the torch. Angus and Ava drag the shelves away from the wall.

'Look!' I say. 'An old door.'

Behind the shelves is a doorway. It's boarded up.

Scrrr-atch.

'Something is behind that door!' says Ava. 'It's creepy.'

Angus gets the broom. 'I'm going to take the board off.' He hits the board with the broom but the board doesn't move. He hits it again.

'Stop,' says Joel. 'There's a hole.'

'Make it bigger,' I say.

'I can do it,' says Ava. She gives the board a karate kick. BANG! The board breaks and there's a big hole now.

Joel shines the torch through the hole. We see a sofa and an old television.

'It's a living room!' I say.

'I'm going in,' says Angus.

Everyone climbs through the hole into the room. In the torch light, we see orange and yellow curtains, green walls and brown carpet on the floor.

'Look at this place!' says Angus. 'Green walls and brown carpet! It's from the 1970s.'

'Hey,' I say. 'Maybe *this* can be our cinema.'

'Yeah,' says Ava. 'That's a great idea. This place is cool.'

'Aargh!' Joel jumps. 'What's that?' He grabs my arm. I jump too, and drop my phone.

'What?'

'Up there.' Joel shines the light up and down. 'There's something on the curtain.'

'What?' says Ava. 'Where?'

'There!' I shout. 'It's jumping off the curtain. It's on the floor.'

'Argh! What is it? What is it?' Everyone is running in circles.

The light hits something in the corner.

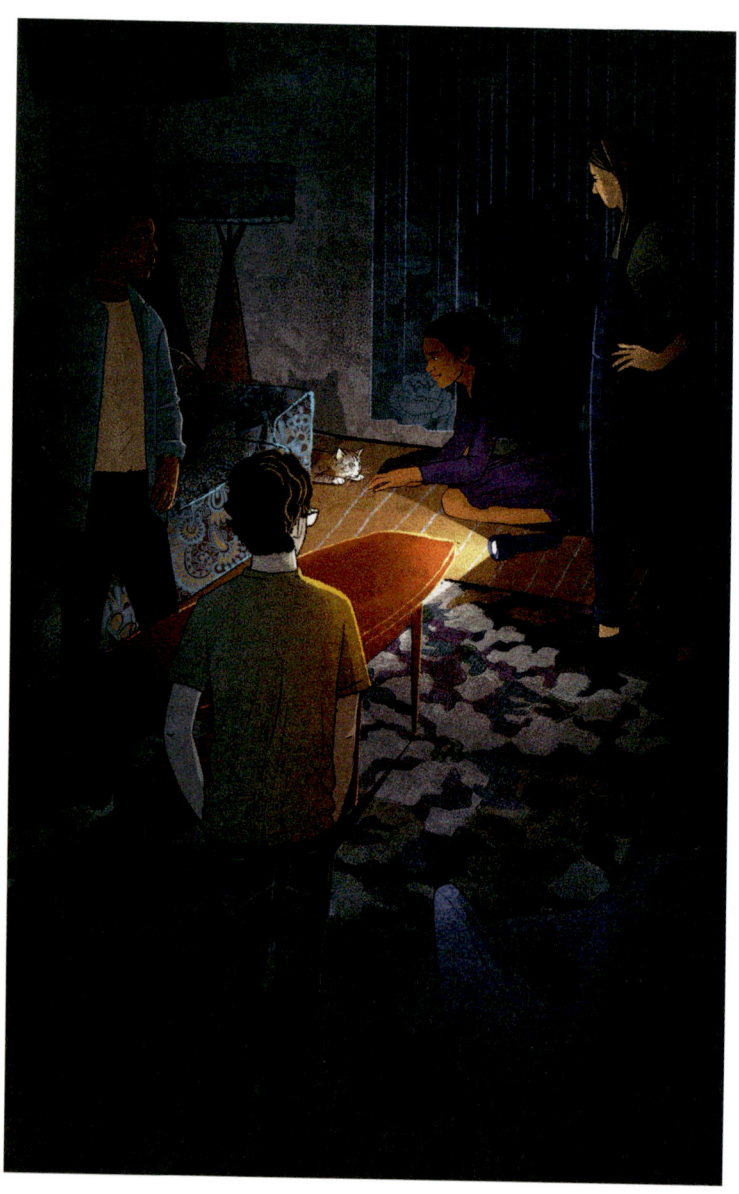

'There!' I shout. I grab the torch from Joel and shine the light into the corner again. 'It's okay. It's okay,' I say. 'It's a cat. It's only a cat.'

I put the torch on the floor and speak quietly. 'Here, Kitty, Kitty, Kitty.'

The cat is small and dirty and scared. *Miaow.* It comes to me and I pick it up. *Miaow.*

Everyone wants to hold it.

'Look at it. It's very thin,' says Ava. 'Hello, Kitty. What are you doing in here? What's your name, eh?'

I hold the cat up to my face. 'You're quick, aren't you, Kitty?' I say. 'You're a rocket.'

'That's a good name,' says Joel. 'Rocket.' He scratches the cat's head. 'Hello, Rocket.'

'Yeah. Hello, Rocket.' Angus puts his nose into the cat's face. 'Hello, Roxy-Woxy. Roxy's very hungry, aren't you?'

'Roxy?' says Joel.

'Yeah,' says Angus. 'Roxy.'

I give him the cat. 'Here, you take Roxy. I've got milk.' I climb through the hole into the shop. I can hear Angus saying, 'Hello, Roxy. Don't be scared.'

I get the milk and an old cup and I'm going to climb through the hole again but there is a sound at the front door. I stop and listen. Two men are talking quietly.

'This is the place.'

'Can you break in, Eddie? Can you?'

'Trevor, I can have this door open in twenty seconds.'

Quickly, I climb through the hole, grab the torch from Ava and turn off the light.

'Shh!' I say. 'Two men are at the front door. They're breaking in!'

Chapter 4
Nice and quiet

I'm scared.

Angus, Ava, Joel and I are behind the sofa in the dark living room. Roxy is drinking milk from the cup. She has to stay quiet. The men are in the shop now. We can hear them.

'Yeah, this place is good, Eddie. Nice and clean. Nice and quiet. The Boss is going to be happy. He's going to love you. You're taking the stuff tomorrow night, Eddie?'

'Tomorrow night, Trevor. Yes, it's a very sad story. At 11.45, I'm sorry to say, there's going to be a break-in at Elite Dresses on Watling Street. They have some very nice dresses in that shop, and tomorrow night …'

The men laugh.

'And you're going to move the stuff here, Eddie?'

'Yeah. To this nice, quiet, empty shop.'

The men are dangerous. We need to call the police but I don't have my phone. Where is it? The room is too dark to see.

'Joel,' I say, very quietly. 'Have you got your phone?'

'No.'

Miaow.

Oh, no. I grab Roxy and look in the cup. It's empty.

'Hey, Eddie, I can hear a cat.'

Oh, no.

'That cat has friends, Trevor. Look at this. Four sleeping bags. A rucksack. Food.'

'The Boss isn't going to like that, is he, Eddie? Is he?'

'Shut your mouth, Trevor.'

I see the light from a torch sweep across the hole.

'Ooh, look, Eddie. There's a hole in the wall.'

The light sweeps over our heads. Oh, no. The men are going to come in! They're going to see us! I hug Roxy. What can we do?

'There's a room in here,' says one of the men. 'Argh! This hole's too small. We need to make it bigger.'

The men hit the wall with something – BANG!

Roxy jumps out of my arms. I can't hold her. Where is she?

The men are in the room now. A light shines into my eyes. I put my hand up to my face. I can't see the man behind the torch.

'Get up,' he says. 'Everyone get up.'

'There are four kids, Eddie.'

Eddie is the man behind the torch.

'Get up,' he says again.

I stand up. I'm very scared. I look at Ava, Joel and Angus. What are we going to do? And where is Roxy?

'Get their torch, Trevor,' says Eddie.

Trevor moves into the light. He has a thin face and small black eyes. He grabs the torch from me and turns it on. The light shines into Eddie's face. I see a big nose and a tattoo.

'Trevor!' he says. 'Put that torch down.'

'Sorry, Eddie.'

'Come out from behind the sofa,' Eddie says to us.

Everyone stands up and comes out.

'And don't move,' says Eddie.

But Angus doesn't listen. He drops to the floor and grabs something. It's my phone! Yes! He can call the police. But he doesn't call them! He's holding up the phone and filming the men.

'You're going to be stars!' Angus says to the men. 'I'm going to put this on YouTube. And in ten seconds, everyone is going to see you.'

'Get the phone,' shouts Eddie. 'Get the phone.'

Trevor grabs at it, but Angus moves. Eddie runs across the room and hits Angus on the arm.

'Argh!' The phone drops to the floor.

Eddie grabs Angus and throws him onto the sofa. 'Stay there!'

Quietly, I move across to the hole in the wall.

Eddie sees me. 'Hey!' He grabs my arm. It hurts.

'You're hurting me,' I say.

'Shut your mouth,' he shouts. He drags me away from the hole.

In the torch light, I see Roxy. She's in the corner, near Eddie, and she's scared. She runs up the curtain behind him.

And she jumps.

'Aargh!' Eddie drops the torch and runs in circles. 'There's something on my head. An animal. Get it off. Get it off! It's scratching my eyes. Get it off!'

'Run!' I shout.

Chapter 5
Let's get out of here!

'Run!' I shout again.

Ava grabs the torch from Trevor. She and Joel run to the hole in the wall. I see Roxy on the floor and I grab her.

'Get my phone,' I say to Angus. He grabs it and we run.

'Stop them!' shouts Eddie.

Ava is in the shop and Joel is climbing through the hole.

I hug Roxy and climb through the hole. But behind me, Angus shouts, 'Marnie! Take the phone!'

Trevor has Angus's leg and Angus is kicking at Trevor.

I grab the phone and call 999.

Joel has the mop. He gives it to Angus.

'Police!' I shout into the phone. 'The old shop at thirty-four Moorbrook Street. Come quickly.'

Angus hits Trevor with the mop and climbs into the shop. But Trevor is quick. He comes through the hole and grabs Angus again.

'Help him!' I shout. But what can I do? I start filming with my phone. 'I'm filming you, Trevor. I'm filming you.'

Ava shines the torch in Trevor's face. Angus kicks him in the leg. But now Eddie is coming through the hole.

'Ava!' I shout. 'Behind you!'

She turns and gives Eddie a karate kick. He drops to the floor. I film everyone.

Joel grabs the mop again and hits him on the head. 'Come out here and I'm going to hit you again,' he says.

Eddie can't come out. 'Trevor!' he shouts.

Trevor drops Angus and runs to the hole. But Joel hits him with the mop. Angus grabs the bucket and throws it over Trevor's head.

'Put him through the hole!' shouts Ava. 'Get the shelves.'

I drop Roxy and my phone onto a sleeping bag and run to help. Joel and Angus throw Trevor in with Eddie. Ava and I drag the shelves across the doorway again.

'Let's get out of here,' says Angus.

I grab Roxy and we run out onto the street. 'Listen, Roxy,' I say. 'The police are coming. I can hear them.'

It's Friday night. Film Club night. And everyone is at The Little Roxy Cinema. Ava, Joel, Ray and Lily are on the sofa and Angus is sitting in a chair with a very big bag of popcorn. Dad and Mr Sims are there too. I'm standing at a small table behind the sofa. There are two projectors on it – one is old and one is new. And I have my laptop.

Roxy sits on a table in the corner. She's clean and fat and she's playing with Angus's feather duster. She lives at the cinema now. She's our Club mascot. I go and stand near her.

'Welcome to The Little Roxy Cinema,' I say.

Everyone cheers.

'Tonight, we're going to see the 1978 film, *The Cat from Outer Space*.'

Everyone cheers again.

'But I have a surprise too – a new short film with a new action star. It's our Club mascot Roxy, in *Roxy Saves the Day*.'

I go to the laptop and hit Play.

Activities

Chapter 1

Before you read

A. Look at the picture on page 5 and circle the correct answers.
1. Where are these people?
    a. in a cinema   b. in a living room   c. in a shed
2. How many young people can you see?
    a. five   b. six   c. seven

B. Find these words in your dictionary. Use them in the sentences.

collect   dusty   shed   carpet

1. Please clean this room. It's very _____!
2. My father likes working in the _____ in the garden.
3. I like the new _____ in this room. It's a nice colour.
4. I _____ old books. I have 367 of them!

C. Listen to Track 3 and answer these questions.
1. What do Marnie and her friends do on Friday nights?
    a. They watch films.   b. They make films.
2. What kind of films do they like?
    a. new films   b. old films
3. Where does Marnie's father keep his films?
    a. in the house   b. in the garden shed

After you read

COMPREHENSION

A. Circle the correct answers.
1. Who doesn't like the old films and film projectors?
    a. Marnie's mother   b. Marnie's father   c. Angus
2. What is the problem with the shed?
    a. It's too old.   b. It's too small.   c. It's too dusty.
3. What does Angus say they need?
    a. a new film projector   b. better films   c. a bigger shed
4. Who does karate?
    a. Lily   b. Ava   c. Joel

B. Circle T for true or F for false for these sentences.
1. Marnie's father likes the idea of a proper little cinema.   T / F
2. Joel says he thinks it's a bad idea.   T / F
3. Mr Sims is a friendly man.   T / F
4. Lily thinks Mr Sims's house is a nice place.   T / F

C. Complete these sentences.
1. Mr Sims has a lot of old houses and _____.
2. Marnie and Angus go to see Mr Sims on _____.
3. When Marnie starts to speak, Mr Sims says she has ten _____.
4. Mr Sims tells them that he doesn't have a _____.

D. Write short answers to these questions.
1. What does Angus think they should call their cinema?
   _____
2. At first, what does Mr Sims do when Marnie and Angus ask him for a building to use?
   _____
3. What film makes Mr Sims stop and remember being a boy at the cinema?
   _____
4. Where does Mr Sims have a shop the film club can use?
   _____

LANGUAGE ACTIVITIES
A. Match the words that go together in Chapter 1.
1. film   pot
2. flower   projector
3. action   shed
4. garden   star

B. Use the letters to spell nouns from Chapter 1. You can find these things in a cinema.
1. harcis _____
2. npcorop _____
3. tcrpae _____
4. iceptur _____

WHAT DO YOU THINK?
Why does Mr Sims decide to let the film club use one of his shops?
_____

Chapter 2

Before you read

A. Look at the picture on page 9 and circle the correct answers.
1. Where do you think Marnie and Angus are?
   a. at school   b. in Marnie's house   c. in the old shop
2. Which word best describes the room?
   a. dirty   b. clean   c. comfortable

B. Find these words in your dictionary. Use them in the sentences.

rubbish   sleepover   shelves   counter

1. In a shop, you pay for things at the _____.
2. In a bookshop, there are lots of books on _____.
3. There's a lot of _____ in the park. Let's clean it up!
4. My friend Sam is having a _____. I'll go there this evening and be back in the morning.

C. Listen to Track 4 and answer these questions.
1. Who opens the door with the key?
   a. Marnie   b. Angus
2. What is on the floor of the shop?
   a. carpet   b. rubbish
3. What does Angus say about the shop?
   a. 'What a mess!'   b. 'I love it!'

After you read

COMPREHENSION

A. Circle the correct answers.
1. What does Angus find at the back of the shop?
   a. a kitchen   b. a bathroom   c. a bedroom
2. When does Marnie want to start cleaning the shop?
   a. on Saturday morning   b. on Saturday afternoon
   c. on Sunday
3. How does Marnie get to the shop in the afternoon?
   a. She walks.   b. She rides a bicycle.   c. Her father drives her.
4. In the afternoon, who arrives at the shop after Marnie?
   a. Ava   b. Ray   c. Lily

B. Circle T for true or F for false for these sentences.
1. Marnie thinks the shop is a good place for their cinema.   T / F
2. When Ava sees the shop, she likes it.   T / F
3. Ray and Lily play football on Saturday afternoon.   T / F
4. Joel arrives with a bucket on his head.   T / F

C. Write short answers to these questions.
1. Where are the friends going to sleep on Saturday night?
   _____
2. What do they bring to sleep in?
   _____
3. Where do they put the rubbish?
   _____
4. At what time do they stop cleaning?
   _____

D. Complete these sentences.
1. The light doesn't turn on because there's no light _____.
2. In the dark, Angus thinks the shop is _____.
3. They sit on their sleeping bags on the _____.
4. For light, they have a torch and their _____.

LANGUAGE ACTIVITIES
A. Match the words that go together in Chapter 2.
1. wash   the sound
2. sweep up   the floor
3. share   the rubbish
4. hear   the food

B. Write the missing vowels in these nouns from Chapter 2. They are all cleaning things.
1. m _ p
2. br _ _ m
3. b _ ck _ t
4. f _ _ th _ r d _ st _ r

WHAT DO YOU THINK?
What do you think the sound is? _____
_____

Chapters 3 and 4

Before you read

A. Answer these questions about the story so far.
1. What are the friends doing in the shop?
   a. staying for the night   b. watching a movie   c. shopping
2. Why does everyone stop talking in the dark shop?
   a. Joel wants to sleep.   b. Angus hears a sound.
   c. Ava asks to them to be quiet.

B. Find these words in your dictionary. Use them in the sentences.

drag   boarded up   hole   grab

1. Can you help me to _____ the table to the window?
2. Don't let the dog run away. _____ him!
3. There's a _____ in the bucket, so it can't hold water.
4. You can't see into the old house because the windows are _____.

C. Listen to Track 5 and answer these questions.
1. What does Joel say he doesn't like?
   a. cats   b. rats
2. Where is the noise coming from?
   a. behind the counter   b. on top of the counter
3. Who says, 'Maybe it's a ghost'?
   a. Angus   b. Joel

After you read

Comprehension

A. Circle the correct answers.
1. What do Angus and Ava drag away from the wall?
   a. the counter   b. the shelves   c. a bag of rubbish
2. How does Angus make the hole in the board?
   a. He hits it with a broom.   b. He kicks it.   c. He scratches it.
3. Who kicks the board to make the hole bigger?
   a. Marnie   b. Joel   c. Ava
4. What do they see when Joel shines the torch through the hole?
   a. a sofa and an old TV   b. a film projector   c. lots of rubbish

B. *Circle T for true or F for false for these sentences.*
1. The things in the living room are old. T / F
2. Marnie thinks the living room could be the cinema. T / F
3. The cat is very big. T / F
4. The cat moves fast. T / F

C. *Complete these sentences.*
1. Marnie thinks the cat moves like a _____.
2. The friends call the cat _____.
3. Marnie gives the cat some _____.
4. When the friends hear the men come in, they hide behind the _____.

D. *Write short answers to these questions.*
1. Where are the men going to put the dresses from Elite Dresses?
   _____
2. How does Eddie know there are people in the old shop?
   _____
3. What does Angus do with Marnie's phone?
   _____
4. Who jumps onto Eddie's head?
   _____

Language activities
A. *Write the correct prepositions in the spaces.*

onto   from   out of   through

1. Everyone climbs _____ the hole into the room.
2. Roxy jumps _____ my arms.
3. He grabs the torch _____ me and turns it on.
4. Eddie grabs Angus and throws him _____ the sofa.

B. *Complete these notes about Trevor and Eddie's faces.*
1. **Trevor:** _____ face, small black _____
2. **Eddie:** big _____, _____

What do you think?
Do you think the friends will be able to get away from Trevor and Eddie? Why or why not?
_____

Chapter 5

Before you read

A. Answer these questions about the story so far.
1. At the end of Chapter 4, where is Marnie's phone?
   a. behind the sofa   b. on the floor   c. in Ava's rucksack
2. What does Roxy do to Eddie?
   a. She jumps on his head.   b. She says *Miaow* to him.
   c. She grabs his leg.

B. Find these words in your dictionary. Use them in the sentences.

   laptop   mascot   cheer   outer space

1. Our football team's _____ is a blue tiger!
2. The people _____ when the team comes out to play.
3. I'm taking my _____ to the library to study.
4. I'd love to travel to _____ one day. Do you think I can?

C. Listen to Track 6 and answer these questions.
1. Who grabs Roxy?
   a. Ava   b. Marnie
2. Who grabs the phone?
   a. Angus   b. Eddie
3. Who grabs Angus's leg?
   a. Trevor   b. Eddie

After you read

Comprehension

A. Circle the correct answers.
1. Who does Marnie call on her phone?
   a. her father   b. Mr Sims   c. the police
2. What does Angus hit Trevor with?
   a. a mop   b. a broom   c. a bucket
3. Who films Trevor and Eddie?
   a. Angus   b. Joel   c. Marnie
4. What does Ava do to Eddie?
   a. She hits him.   b. She kicks him.   c. She grabs him.

B. *Circle T for true or F for false for these sentences.*
1. Trevor throws a bucket over Angus's head.   T / F
2. The friends close up the doorway and shut Trevor
   and Eddie into the living room.   T / F
3. Marnie puts Roxy and her phone into a sleeping bag.   T / F
4. The friends all run out onto the street.   T / F

C. *Complete these sentences.*
1. On Film Club night, Ava, Joel, Ray and Lily sit on the
   _____.
2. Angus has a bag of _____.
3. Roxy plays with Angus's _____.
4. To show films, the club has an old projector, a new projector and Marnie's _____.

D. *Write short answers to these questions.*
1. Who comes to watch a film with the club on Friday night?
   _____

2. Who is the club's mascot?
   _____

3. What 1978 film is the club going to watch?
   _____

4. What is the name of Marnie's new film?
   _____

LANGUAGE ACTIVITIES
A. *Match the words that go together in Chapter 5.*
1. shine   the shelves
2. call   Play
3. drag   999
4. hit   the torch

B. *Write the missing vowels in these adjectives from Chapter 5.*
1. f _ t   3. q _ _ ck
2. cl _ _ n   4. sh _ rt

WHAT DO YOU THINK?
Do you think Roxy is going to have a good life as the mascot of the Film Club? Why or why not?
_____

Glossary

adj. adjective; *adv.* adverb; *excl.* exclamation; *n.* noun; *prep.* preposition; *pron.* pronoun; *v.* verb

across /əˈkrɒs/ *adv., prep.*	über, durch; hinüber
along /əˈlɒŋ/ *prep.*	entlang
away from /əweɪ frɒm/ *adv., prep.*	weg von
bathroom /ˈbɑːθˌruːm/ *n.*	Toilette
bigger /ˈbɪgə/ *adj.*	größer
board /bɔːd/ *n.*	Brett
boarded up /ˌbɔːdɪd ˈʌp/ *adj.*	mit Brettern vernagelt
boss /bɒs/ *n.*	Boss, Chef/in
break-in /ˈbreɪk ˌɪn/ *n.*	Einbruch
break in /ˌbreɪk ˈɪn/ *v.*	einbrechen
broom /bruːm/ *n.*	Besen
bucket /ˈbʌkɪt/ *n.*	Eimer
carpet /ˈkɑːpɪt/ *n.*	Teppich
cheer /tʃɪə/ *v.*	jubeln, applaudieren
circle /ˈsɜːkl/ *n.*	Kreis
clean /kliːn/ *v.*	putzen
climb /klaɪm/ *v.*	klettern, steigen
collect /kəˈlekt/ *v.*	sammeln
corner /ˈkɔːnə/ *n.*	Ecke
counter /ˈkaʊntə/ *n.*	Theke, Tresen
creepy /kriːpi/ *adj.*	gruselig, unheimlich
curtain /ˈkɜːtn/ *n.*	Vorhang
doorway /ˈdɔːˌweɪ/ *n.*	Tür, Türöffnung
drag /dræg/ *v.*	ziehen, schleppen
drive /draɪv/ *v.*	fahren
drop /drɒp/ *v.*	(sich) fallen lassen
dust /dʌst/ *v.*	abstauben
dusty /ˈdʌsti/ *adj.*	staubig
empty /ˈempti/ *adj.*	leer, leerstehend

feather duster /ˌfeðə ˈdʌstə/ *n.*	Staubwedel
film projector /fɪlm prəˈdʒektə/ *n.*	Filmprojektor
flower pot /ˈflaʊəˌpɒt/ *n.*	Blumentopf
get (something) off /ˌget (sʌmθɪŋ) ˈɒf/ *v.*	wegmachen, abbekommen
get up /ˌget ˈʌp/ *v.*	aufstehen
ghost /gəʊst/ *n.*	Geist
grab (at) /ˈgræb (ət)/ *v.*	greifen (nach), packen
great /greɪt/ *adj.*	großartig, toll
hit /hɪt/ *v.*	schlagen, treffen (auf)
hold /həʊld/ *v.*	halten
hole /həʊl/ *n.*	Loch
hug /hʌg/ *n.*	Umarmung
v.	umarmen
hungry /ˈhʌŋgri/ *adj.*	hungrig
key /kiː/ *n.*	Schlüssel
kick /kɪk/ *v.*	treten
n.	Kick, Tritt
light bulb /ˈlaɪt ˌbʌlb/ *n.*	Glühbirne
look for /ˌlʊk fə/ *v.*	suchen nach
mascot /ˈmæskɒt/ *n.*	Maskottchen
mess /mes/ *n.*	Durcheinander, Unordnung
mop /mɒp/ *n.*	Mopp, Wischer
need /niːd/ *v.*	brauchen, müssen
newspaper /ˈnjuːzˌpeɪpə/ *n.*	Zeitung
out of /aʊt əv/ *prep.*	aus, weg von
outer space /ˌaʊtə ˈspeɪs/ *n.*	Weltraum
plastic bag /ˈplæstɪk ˌbæg/ *n.*	Plastiktüte
proper /ˈprɒpə/ *adj.*	richtig, ordentlich
quick /kwɪk/ *adj.*	schnell
quickly /ˈkwɪkli/ *adv.*	schnell
quiet /ˈkwaɪət/ *adj.*	leise, ruhig
quietly /ˈkwaɪətli/ *adv.*	leise, ruhig
rat /ræt/ *n.*	Ratte
remember /rɪˈmembə/ *v.*	sich erinnern

rocket /ˈrɒkɪt/ *n.*	Rakete
rubbish /ˈrʌbɪʃ/ *n.*	Müll, Dreck
save /seɪv/ *v.*	retten
scared /skeəd/ *adj.*	verängstigt, verschreckt
scratch /skrætʃ/ *v.*	kratzen, kraulen
share /ʃeə/ *v.*	teilen
shed /ʃed/ *n.*	Hütte, Schuppen
shelf /ʃelf/ *n.*	Regal
shine /ʃaɪn/ *v.*	scheinen, leuchten
sleeping bag /ˈsliːpɪŋ ˌbæg/ *n.*	Schlafsack
sleepover /ˈsliːpˌəʊvə/ *n.*	Pyjamaparty
sound /saʊnd/ *n.*	Geräusch
stay /steɪ/ *v.*	bleiben
stuff /stʌf/ *n.*	Sachen, Zeug
surprise /səˈpraɪz/ *n.*	Überraschung
sweep (up) /ˌswiːp (ˈʌp)/ *v.*	(auf)fegen, (auf)wischen; streichen
through /θruː/ *prep.*	durch
throw /θrəʊ/ *v.*	werfen
tired /ˈtaɪəd/ *adj.*	müde
tool /tuːl/ *n.*	Werkzeug
torch /tɔːtʃ/ *n.*	Taschenlampe
turn /tɜːn/ *v.*	(sich) drehen
turn on/off /ˌtɜːn ˈɒn/ɒf/ *v.*	einschalten / ausschalten
wash /wɒʃ/ *v.*	waschen, putzen
yuk /jʌk/ *excl.*	igitt

The Little Roxy Cinema Activities: Answer Key

Chapter 1
Before you read
A. 1. c, 2. b   B. 1. dusty, 2. shed, 3. carpet, 4. collect
C. 1. a, 2. b, 3. b

After you read
Comprehension
A. 1. a, 2. b, 3. c, 4. b   B. 1. T, 2. F, 3. F, 4. F   C. 1. shops, 2. Saturday (morning), 3. seconds, 4. cinema
D. 1. The Angus McTavish Cinema, 2. He shuts the window, 3. *The 5000 Fingers of Dr T*, 4. on Moorbrook Street

Language activities
A. 1. film projector, 2. flower pot, 3. action star, 4. garden shed
B. 1. chairs, 2. popcorn, 3. carpet, 4. picture

What do you think?
Students' own answers

Chapter 2
Before you read
A. 1. c, 2. a   B. 1. counter, 2. shelves, 3. rubbish, 4. sleepover   C. 1. b, 2. b, 3. a

After you read
Comprehension
A. 1. b, 2. b, 3. c, 4. a   B. 1. T, 2. T, 3. T, 4. F   C. 1. in the shop, 2. sleeping bags, 3. in (plastic) bags, 4. six o'clock
D. 1. bulb, 2. creepy, 3. floor, 4. phones

Language activities
A. 1. wash the floor, 2. sweep up the rubbish, 3. share the food, 4. hear the sound   B. 1. mop, 2. broom, 3. bucket, 4. feather duster

What do you think?
Students' own answers

Chapters 3 and 4
Before you read
A. 1. a, 2. b   B. 1. drag, 2. grab, 3. hole, 4. boarded up
C. 1. b, 2. a, 3. b

After you read
Comprehension
A. 1. b, 2. a, 3. c, 4. a   B. 1. T, 2. T, 3. F, 4. T   C. 1. rocket, 2. Roxy, 3. milk, 4. sofa
D. 1. In the old shop, 2. He sees the sleeping bags, rucksack and food. 3. He films the man. 4. Roxy

Language activities
A. 1. through, 2. out of, 3. from, 4. onto
B. 1. Trevor: thin face, small black eyes, 2. Eddie: big nose, tattoo

What do you think?
Students' own answers

Chapter 5
Before you read
A. 1. b, 2. a   B. 1. mascot, 2. cheer, 3. laptop, 4. outer space
C. 1. b, 2. a, 3. a

After you read
Comprehension
A. 1. c, 2. a, 3. c, 4. b   B. 1. F, 2. T, 3. T, 4. T   C. 1. sofa, 2. popcorn, 3. feather duster, 4. laptop
D. 1. Marnie's father and Mr Sims, 2. Roxy, 3. *The Cat from Outer Space*, 4. *Roxy Saves the Day*

Language activities
A. 1. shine the torch, 2. call 999, 3. drag the shelves, 4. hit Play
B. 1. fat, 2. clean, 3. quick, 4. short

What do you think?
Students' own answers